ANIMALS in DANGER

Giant Panda

Rod Theodorou

Heinemann
LIBRARY

H www.heinemann.co.uk
Visit our website to find out more information about **Heinemann Library** books.

To order:
☎ Phone 44 (0) 1865 888066
🖹 Send a fax to 44 (0) 1865 314091
💻 Visit the Heinemann Bookshop at www.heinemann.co.uk to browse our catalogue and order online.

First published in Great Britain by Heinemann Library, Halley Court, Jordan Hill, Oxford OX2 8EJ, a division of Reed Educational and Professional Publishing Ltd. Heinemann is a registered trademark of Reed Educational & Professional Publishing Limited.

OXFORD MELBOURNE AUCKLAND JOHANNESBURG BLANTYRE
GABORONE IBADAN PORTSMOUTH NH (USA) CHICAGO

Designed by Ron Kamen
Illustrations by Dewi Morris/Robert Sydenham
Originated by Ambassador Litho Ltd.
Printed by South China Printing in Hong Kong / China

ISBN 0431 00134 0 (hardback)
04 03 02 01 00
10 9 8 7 6 5 4 3 2 1

British Library Cataloguing in Publication Data
Theodorou, Rod
    Giant panda. - (Animals in danger)
    1.Giant panda - Juvenile literature 2.Endangered species - Juvenile literature
    I.Title
    599.7'89

Acknowledgements
The Publishers would like to thank the following for permission to reproduce photographs:
Ardea London: Jean-Paul Ferrero pg.11, Adrian Warren pg.18; *BBC Natural History Unit*: Lynn M Stone pg.14, pg.17, Sue Flood pg.22; *FLPA*: Eichhorn Zingel pg.4, Gerard Lacz pg.4, B Lea & Dembinsky pg.7, Fritz Polking pg.9, E & D Hosking pg.12, pg.27, Leeson Sunset pg.13; *Holt Studios*: Nigel Cattlin pg.25; *Mike Johnson*: pg.4; *NHPA*: Henry Ausloos pg.23, Andy Rouse pg.26; *Oxford Scientific Films*: Bates Littlehales pg.5, Jim Tuten pg.8, Keren Su pg.16, Ralph R Reinhold; *Still Pictures*: Julio Etchart pg.6, pg.24, Putao pg.20; *WWF Photolibrary*: Susan A Mainka pg.15, G Schaller pg.19.

Cover photograph reproduced with permission of Oxford Scientific Films.

Our thanks to Henning Dräger WWF-UK for his comments in the preparation of this book.

Every effort has been made to contact copyright holders of any material reproduced in this book. Any omissions will be rectified in subsequent printings if notice is given to the Publisher.

Contents

Any words appearing in the text in bold, **like this**, are explained in the Glossary.

Animals in danger

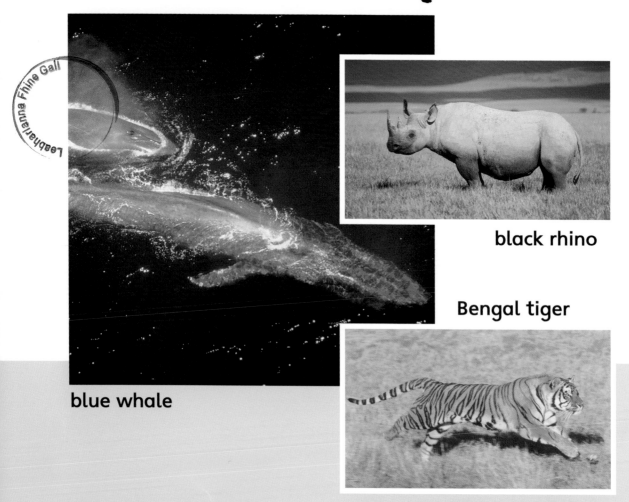

black rhino

Bengal tiger

blue whale

All over the world, more than 10,000 animal **species** are in danger. Some are in danger because their home is being **destroyed.** Many are in danger from people hunting them.

This book is about giant pandas and why they are in danger. Unless people look after them, they will become **extinct.** We will only be able to find out about them from books like this.

What are giant pandas?

Giant pandas are large **mammals**. They live in the mountains of China where the right types of plants grow for the pandas to feed on. Pandas are very important to the people of China.

For a long time, scientists thought giant pandas were part of the bear family. Now they think they have their own family, which is closer to **raccoons** than bears.

What do giant pandas look like?

Giant pandas look like bears and have thick black and white fur, and a short tail. Their ears, legs, shoulders and the fur around their eyes are black. The rest of the fur on their body is white.

Giant pandas can see well. They have strong jaws and teeth for chewing tough food. They have special bones like thumbs to help them hold their food.

Where do giant pandas live?

CHINA

Key: ■ where giant pandas live

Giant pandas live only in six small areas of China. They live in the mountain areas around the centre and southwest of the country.

Giant pandas live high up in the mountains, in cool forests full of **bamboo** plants. There are clouds, rain and mist here throughout the year.

11

What do giant pandas eat?

Giant pandas eat **bamboo** plants. They eat the woody, tough stem and roots but they like the green leaves best.

Bamboo is not very **nutritious**, so the giant panda has to eat for 10 to 16 hours a day to stay fit and healthy.

Giant panda babies

Giant pandas are very shy and they like to live on their own. The **males** and **females** only meet in late spring or early summer to **mate**.

Three to five months later the female may give birth to one or two babies, called cubs, in a **den** in the ground. Usually only one of the cubs will live to become fully grown.

Looking after the cubs

When giant panda cubs are born they are very small and helpless. They cannot see, and they have very little fur. The cubs drink their mother's milk for about six months.

The cubs grow quite slowly. They can move around after three months. After about a year they will go to live on their own. Giant pandas live between 17 and 20 years in the wild.

Unusual giant panda facts

The giant panda has a special bone on each of its front paws that it uses like a thumb to hold the **bamboo** as it eats.

The giant panda used to eat meat but a long time ago it changed to mostly eating plants. We now know that sometimes it will also eat small **mammals,** fish and birds.

How many giant pandas are there?

One hundred years ago there were large numbers of giant pandas in China. Now there are less than 700 of them in the wild, even though they are **protected** by **law**.

Nowadays the giant pandas in China live mainly in 13 special protected areas, called **reserves**. The pandas can live safely in the reserves because people cannot hunt them.

Why is the giant panda in danger?

Giant pandas are in danger from people. They can get caught in mountain traps set by people that are meant to catch other animals, like musk deer and black bears.

Hunters in China try to kill pandas to sell their fur for coats. If the hunters are caught they face being punished with the **death penalty**.

Why is the giant panda in danger?

Giant pandas are in danger because their **habitat** is being **destroyed**. Forest areas are being cut down to make room for homes and factories. The trees are sold as wood for building and furniture.

Sometimes the **bamboo** plants that the giant pandas eat come into flower. This means that the pandas cannot eat them. They have to move home or they starve.

How is the giant panda being helped?

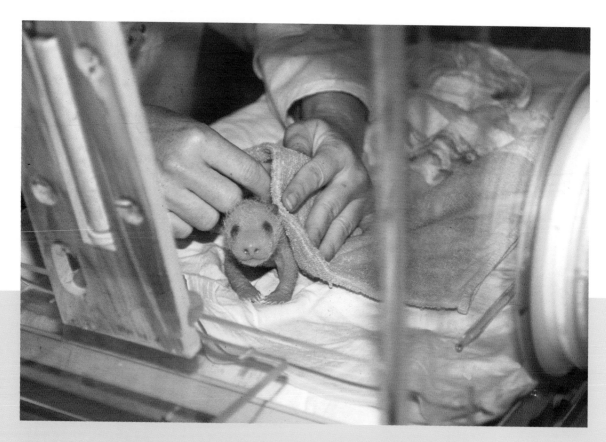

Conservation groups work to protect the pandas in the **reserves**. Sometimes the conservation workers look after and raise baby pandas if the mother cannot.

The conservation groups work with local people to stop animals being hunted or caught in traps. Some pandas **mate** and have babies in zoos. They are then set free into the wild.

Giant panda factfile

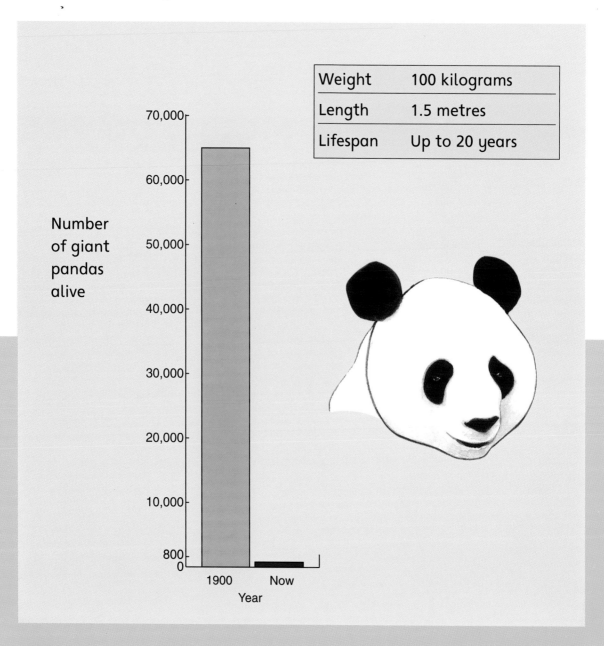

Weight	100 kilograms
Length	1.5 metres
Lifespan	Up to 20 years

Number of giant pandas alive

70,000
60,000
50,000
40,000
30,000
20,000
10,000
800
0

1900   Now
Year

World danger table

	Number that may have been alive 100 years ago	Number that may be alive today
Bengal tiger	100,000	4500
Blue whale	335,000	4000
Black rhino	1,000,000	2000
Mountain gorilla	85,000	500
Florida manatee	75,000	1400

There are thousands of other animals in the world that are in danger of becoming **extinct**. This table shows some of these animals.

Can you find out more about them?

Further reading, addresses and websites

Books

People or Wildlife? Earth Watch series, Terry Jennings, A & C Black, 1992

Pandas, Picture Library series, Norman Barett, Franklin Watts, 1996

Pandas, Wildlife at Risk series, Gillian Standring, Wayland, 1991

The Atlas of Endangered Species, John A. Burton, David and Charles, 1991

Vanishing Species, Green Issues series, Miles Barton, Franklin Watts, 1997

Organizations

Friends of the Earth: UK - 26-28 Underwood Street, London, N1 7JQ ☎ (020) 7490 1555 Australia - 312 Smith Street, Collingwood, Vic 3065 ☎ 03 9419 8700

Greenpeace: UK - Canonbury Villas, London, N1 2PN ☎ (020) 7865 8100 Australia - Level 4, 39 Liverpool Street, Sydney, NSW 2000 ☎ 02 9261 4666

WWF: UK - Panda House, Weyside Park, Catteshall Lane, Godalming, Surrey, GU7 1XR ☎ (01483) 426 444 Australia - Level 5, 725 George Street, Sydney, NSW 2000 ☎ 02 9281 5515

Useful Websites

www.bbc.co.uk/nature/

The BBC's animals site. Go to Really Wild for information on all sorts of animals, including fun activities, the latest news, and links to programmes.

www.defenders.org

A conservation group dedicated to protecting animals and plants. Go to Kids Planet on their site.

www.fonz.org

Friends of the Natural Zoo. A conservation site supporting the American Smithsonian Natural Zoo in Washington D.C.

www.giant-panda.com

Amazing photos of giant pandas and their young.

www.sandiegozoo.org

The world-famous American San Diego Zoo's site. Go to the Pick an Animal section for games and factsheets.

www.wwf.org

The World Wildlife Fund For Nature (WWF) is the world's largest independent conservation organization. The WWF conserves wildlife and the natural environment for present and future generations.

Glossary

bamboo	a type of plant with long stems and green leaves
conservation	looking after things, especially if they are in danger
death penalty	when a person is killed as a punishment for doing something wrong
den	place where wild animals live or hide
destroyed	spoilt, broken or torn apart so it can't be used
extinct	a species that has completely died out and can never live again
females	the opposite of a male, such as a girl or woman
habitats	the home or place where something lives
law	a rule or something you have to do
males	the opposite of a female, such as a boy or man
mammals	warm-blooded animals, like humans, that feed their young on their mother's milk
mate	when a male animal and a female animal come together to make young
nutritious	when a food is healthy and good for you
protected	looked after, sometimes by law
racoons	small mammal, with a bushy tail with black and white rings
reserve	a large, protected area where the animals are looked after by guards
species	a group of living things that are very similar

Index

Titles in the *Animals in Danger* series include:

Hardback   0 431 00129 4

Hardback   0 431 00128 6

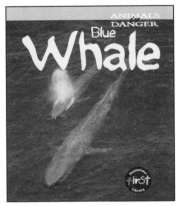

Hardback   0 431 00130 8

Hardback   0 431 00133 2

Hardback   0 431 00134 0

Hardback   0 431 00126 X

Find out about the other titles in this series on our website www.heinemann.co.uk/library